Enter Venus

By Tanya Ochoa

Thank you to those who've shown me what it's like to be loved and thank you to those who've shown me that, not everyone will love me.

Copyright © 2020 by Tanya Ochoa

All rights reserved. No part of this book may be reproduced or used in any manner without written permission of the copyright owner except for the use of quotations in a book review.

Book design by Markus Spisk and Tanya Ochoa

ISBN 978-1-79483-939-7 (paperback)

Printed in the United States of America

GL

Who am I to believe you only need me?

When you live in a sea

Of a thousand beautiful creatures

Who yearn to stand

Where I want to be

It's 3 am

I can't sleep

How many verses start this way?

You make me feel this constant repetition of infatuation and self-sabotage

It comes and goes

In a circle

So, it never really

Goes

I'm orbiting around the idea that there might be hope

A vulture waiting for the moment the wounded takes its last breath

Even if you pay no mind to me

My self-absorbed mind believes there is a thread of hope

I cling to it

As if

If I were to let go

I'd be damned for not trying

No es cualquier cosa

Decirte que te quiero

Cuando me cuesta tanto

Sentir algo así

No pasa cada día

Ni cada mes

Pero cada vez que intento

Demostrar lo que siento

La respuesta sigue igual

Y se convierten en fantasma

You smell like fresh rain

In the morning

And like the grass

I soak it up

I can't seem to get enough of you

Will I ever tire from loving you?

Uncertainty

Blissfully unaware of how you feel

                        It's a lie I tell myself is real

                        No bliss in this confusion

I want you

And that's all there is to know

Daydream

My sea of imagination

Floods with constant admiration

I wish I could see what the future has in store for us

I hide these little moments inside a mason jar

So, when I pull them out

I'll get to see you smile

Won't you stay a while?

Even if it's not for me

Make up an excuse

To sit

Right next to me

Insecurity

Every move I make is a call for attention

Not everyone's

Just his

His attention

On me

When deprived

I fluster

I wait

I tear myself apart

Picking at the pieces that clearly fit

But my eyes distort

What should I fix? What needs rearranging? What suits his needs?

The slightest glance at me is enough

Conversations with him are a blessing

I'm hopeless

He doesn't want me

But my brain refuses to register this

No, it must be a misunderstanding

Who doesn't love a beautiful mess?

<u>Last Name</u>

Bury yourself in me

And leave a scar

So, I never forget

What you felt like

<u>Yes</u>

                    When the night is over

Will you still want me?

                    When I've given you what you want

Will you still crave me?

Your Name

I like seeing your name

On the black/white flip page

Knowing I'll be seeing you soon

My cheeks flush like a sunset in June

When I'm around you

I feel at my worst

Shaking and breathing

Like my lungs are to burst

But you don't seem to notice

I don't think you know it

I'm falling for you

Answer

My heart's knocking

Waiting for you

To answer the door

I could make use of this time

But everything else seems to be such a bore

What is a future?

What is my past?

I seem to forget all of these things

At last

<u>Sin</u>

Incinerate my insecurities

If you insist on igniting my suspicions

Manifest your true intentions

Before I give way to your sculpted silhouette

Release me from the hand you hold me in

If you don't want to hold mine

Fallback

Why do you keep me here

When you're unsure of where we lie

Extinguish my paralyzing thoughts

Help me connect the dots

So, I can move with you

The way you want me to

Where do we fall in line?

Do I cross your mind?

Or is this the only time?

When our bodies intertwine

I know what I signed up for

Can you show me how to stop craving more

M

I don't want to secrete every secret of mine

        Until I am no mystery to the foreign eye

I don't want to lose myself in another's labyrinth mind

        With my beliefs and words left behind

I don't want to fade away

        Destroying my frail ambitions made of clay

I don't want to die

        Without a second try

I apologize for the monstrosities my mind comes up with

When I think of you

And most of all

Telling you

The atrocities of my words escape my lips when I least expect it

I cannot control their impulse

And I'm sorry

For telling you how much I want you

When I know

You don't feel the same

I hate that I'm fragile

So shallow and alone

Wish I could get rid of these feelings that drag my sanity along

I'm going crazy

Repeating

The same thoughts in my head

A part of me just wishes

I were

dead

Life's filled with antidepressants

Blacking out any thought of you filled with resentment

I wish you knew how much I think about you when you're gone

But I know I don't cross your mind at all

I promise I'll shut up when I'm not so broken up about it

I promise I'll stop buying things with hidden meaning behind it

I promise I'll stop writing letters with hopelessness inside it

I know you see how hard I'm trying

Well I'm fucking sick of crying

These feelings I'm repressing, I'll just keep denying

When the light parts the sky

    I wonder if you think of me

When the songs I share, play

    I wonder if you long for me

When the rain hits your window as you lay in bed

    I wonder if you remember late night talks with me

When you walk down a crowded street

    I wonder if you wish I was there to hold your hand

When you're by yourself and venom fills your thoughts

    I wonder

        If you wish it was I

            That polluted your very being

<u>2-line</u>

I'm alone with my thoughts

But all I think about is you

Do I desire you

Or just the thought of having you

I feel happiest being around you

But could it be

That I am a somber waste of space

That appreciates a good thing

When it's there

Possibly the most difficult thing about existence is

Figuring out what our feelings intend for us

Because

        we

                are

                        not

                                  in control of what we feel

D

My heart is filled with joy

As if molten gold were being pumped within my arteries

This gold weighs not

But only lifts my spirits

You are the songs that live within my bloodstream

The violins that replace my veins

You play the untouched strings no one has dared to find

I've got an insatiable desire for your presence

A day without you

Is a day wasted

You bring about a happiness that has been dormant for so long

I see no malice in your pitch black eyes

But a comfort within the shadow's home

I want to rest there

It is as if I am seeing you through brand-new eyes

Your gaze is a gateway to my hyper-active heart

Your smile fills any doubt of negativity I ever had

My cheeks can't help but flush at the very sight of you

Your kindness is an art form

That I cannot seem to imitate

Here's a toast

To the loves I may never have

For it is through them

That I will continue to suffer

Dark clouds linger around me

I cannot seem to find the thing I am supposed to be searching for

I want to weep in the arms of a marble statue

Carved to perfection by my imagination

Who hands me paper flowers

For every tear I shed

I know a flawless figure is an unreasonable desire

But when you've spent your whole life trying, to a tire

How can there not be someone out there made just this way

Your lips are purgatory

Between the earth and the sky

With hell's fire raging in your eyes

Your heart's made of papier-mâché

That's paved a way to heaven's gates

Time is of no importance

Tracing the outlines of your stained glass skin

When doubt has died

Won't you let me in?

You read my body as if it is no foreign language

Your touch wavers my composure

The words we have to say are infinite

So, we remain silent in its stead

Grandeur

When I look at you

It is as if I am standing before the sun

And somehow

I'm not being disintegrated

You radiate a warmth that seeps into my core

And I never want to leave your side

Your laugh is my greatest reward

Your smile, a trophy

A symbol of my triumph

A golden emblem that's burned into my mind

So, let me be the moon you hide behind when you feel the need to rest from your never-ending efforts to give the world life

The skies have kissed your entirety and wrapped you in its clouds to hold you when I'm not there

Tell me you've missed me when I return from a minute's journey across the room

Let us plunge into velvet blankets without words

Swinging to the songs of the wind between our fingers

Let me show you a life where your mistakes matter not

But only the way you choose to live presently

And then there's you

The one my eyes lean toward

As if they were born to do just that

They lower in dissatisfaction

Wishing to inch closer

Knowing I'd be imposed by never ending obstacles

My heart weighs heavy when you're gone

As if gravity makes it a point to remind me

That it too exists

I'm just waiting for the leaves to die

So, I may watch you walk among the stars

If I may be so bold as the neon light within your eyes

I'd have a body embraced in an endless array of scars

To have you is a mosaic of desire

Composed of your words; broken mirror shards

If your heart yearns for mine

Take me without question

Don't mind the whispers of the outside world's aggression

I envy the ocean as it gives color to the sky

Interlacing my fingers with clouds the shape of your hand

Only to be awakened by the burst of a bubble

I wish I could breathe you in like smoke

To have you in my lungs forever

Is it bad, that when I sleep

My thoughts confuse real-life with dreams

So, when I wake

I cannot tell if you proclaimed

You felt the same

The night feels off without you

As if you are what keeps my night intact

The pillow beneath me whispers songs in the shape of your voice

The silence is numbing

As I have nothing to imagine

I

    Drift

        Into

            Slumber

I dream in milk and honey, what stirs in my chest when you speak to me

I want you to drink from my lips, the prettiest words I can spew

Let me know if they're good enough for you

Me

<u>October 20, 2019</u>

Hello

My name is Tanya

I'm 20 years old

I am loved by many

I feel it in my chest

I feel it in the way my face relaxes when I'm alone

I don't feel alone even if I'm on my own

I can finally let those anxious thoughts rest

I see what those I love would do for me

And they know what I would do for them

They feel my love

I feel theirs

It is the feeling that stitches me together

Preventing me from coming undone

A crime of passion

These dreams of mine are a crime to stability and certainty

These dreams of mine are pure passion and dignified

The future holds so much for me

I fear it may break its shelf

Self-doubt is my only set back

I have the support of the world at my disposal

I fear nothing but fear itself

I've found happiness within myself

I looked for it in others when I loathed the body I came in

I looked for it in a lover who later made my psyche loathe some more

I looked for it in ones I couldn't have

Unreachable works of art

I found happiness in myself

Where only I could provide what others couldn't